The Nature for Toddlers Activity Book

THE
Nature for Toddlers
ACTIVITY BOOK

50 Fun Early Learning Activities
to Explore the Natural World

JENETTE RESTIVO

ROCKRIDGE
PRESS

TO MY BOYS, ZANE AND CALVIN, AND THEIR
FELLOW WILD NATURE CRITTERS

First Rockridge Press trade paperback edition 2022

Rockridge Press and the Rockridge Press logo are trademarks or registered trademarks of Callisto Media Inc. and/or its affiliates in the United States and other countries and may not be used without written permission.

For general information on our other products and services, please contact our Customer Care Department within the United States at (866) 744-2665, or outside the United States at (510) 253-0500.

Paperback ISBN: 978-1-68539-735-7 | eBook ISBN: 979-8-88608-834-2

Manufactured in the United States of America

Interior and Cover Designer: Jennifer Hsu
Art Producer: Sue Bischofberger
Editor: Laura Bryn Sisson
Production Editor: Emily Sheehan
Production Manager: David Zapanta

Illustrations used under license from shutterstock.com
Author photo courtesy of Joel Gardner

10 9 8 7 6 5 4 3 2 1 0

Contents

CHAPTER 3:

Learning about Earth: Soil, Rocks, and Water 25

CHAPTER 4:

Creatures and Critters: Birds, Bugs, and More 43

CHAPTER 5:

Green Growers: Flowers, Leaves, and Trees 61

CHAPTER 1

Before You Explore

The outside world is a wonderfully stimulating place for a toddler to explore. The smells, sights, sounds, and textures offer a sensory smorgasbord to enrich your child's growing brain. Toddlers are curious, playful, and ready and willing to take in new experiences and explore their world. That's why the first three years of life are the perfect time to introduce your child to nature play!

Digging in mud, planting seeds, balancing on a log, splashing in puddles, and scribbling with sticks are all fantastic fun for a toddler, but these activities also help foster a toddler's physical development. The activities in this book are designed to delight toddlers and inspire learning through outdoor play in nature. Your toddler will develop physical, creative, fine motor, and language skills in a fun, age-appropriate way when engaging with the natural world.

My Toddler-Parenting Nature Adventure

When my oldest son was a toddler, he started noticing everything about the world. And he was eager to explore it. With such curiosity and boundless energy, I wondered how I was going to keep him busy! I found my answer right outside our door. Whenever I took my son outside, a transformation happened. He was calmer and more engaged. Whether he was digging in our garden or filling and dumping his mini wheelbarrow, nature play never bored him. As often as I could, I took him, and later his younger brother, into nature.

Many years later, they still love being outdoors. I like to say that my boys were raised with nature. I strongly believe in the importance of experiencing nature in childhood, and I hope that the ideas in this book help your toddler fall in love with nature.

Benefits of Nature Play

Nature is good for us in mind, body, and spirit. By observing, exploring, collecting, sorting, or just being outside, a toddler learns and develops in so many ways.

The feel of soft moss underfoot. The comfort of a soft breeze. The clean smell of pine. The best strategy for walking on a log. Nature offers a sensory buffet, building nerve connections in a toddler's brain that help with complex learning tasks, language development, cognitive growth, fine and gross motor skills, problem-solving, and social interaction.

As toddlers grow curious about critters in nature, they will learn new words. As they explore how their bodies interact with logs or puddles, they will learn balance, coordination, and orientation. As they play in mud, toddlers build a stronger immune system. When you add natural elements to a child's play space, they show more variety in their movement.

But one of my favorite benefits of nature play is that it helps develop more nature-connected kids. The more we know about and understand nature, the more we want to protect it. This is true at any age.

Toddler Time

The nature play activities in this book are designed to offer fun ideas for exploring nature with your child so they'll want to return outdoors over and over again!

When engaging in the activities, always be flexible. Follow the steps as best you can, but remember that toddlers are spontaneous little people who often have their own plans. Feel free to let your toddler improvise. If they are more interested in throwing rocks in the pond rather than collecting rocks, that's nature play, too. The important thing is that your toddler is observing, interacting, exploring, and *enjoying* their time in nature.

Whenever you set out to engage in nature play with your toddler, remember that you are your toddler's best teacher. When you model comfort and interest in nature, your toddler will learn that, too. Aim to spend time outside in nature with your child as often as you can, in any season.

Because nature play offers so many benefits to your toddler, they will be learning and developing all the time. Each activity in this book engages one or more developmental skills, which are represented on the following page. Feel free to use the icons to select activities based on the skill or skills you want to focus on.

SKILLS LEARNED

This list features crucial skills that the activities in this book can help your toddler develop. Each activity will include icons representing the different skills the activity can engage.

asking
questions

cause and
effect

classifying
and sorting

fine motor
skills

gross motor
skills

imagination

ABC

language and
vocabulary

listening

noticing and
identifying

problem
solving

SAFETY FIRST!

It's important to ensure your toddler is always safely engaging in the activities in this book. Take into consideration the "Caution" notes included with certain activities where there may be a safety risk.

Here are some general safety guidelines when engaging in any nature play activity with your toddler:

1. Toddlers require constant adult supervision. This is critical and always the best safety precaution. Young children should never be left unattended outdoors or anywhere.

2. Toddlers often put objects in their mouths. When working with loose parts in nature, such as stones or pine cones, always watch your toddler! If the object can fit through a toilet paper tube, it poses a choking hazard. Always pay close attention so they do not put berries or plants in their mouths because some are poisonous.

3. Toddlers can drown if they fall into even a few inches of water in a container. Always closely supervise when your toddler is around water. Never leave them unattended around bins, buckets, or pools of water.

4. Toddlers are still unsteady on their feet. Keep close to your toddler, especially near water, hills, or rough terrain, where they could stumble or fall.

5. Watch your toddler closely when they are playing with sticks. They should choose a stick without splinters or sharp, pointy edges, and it should be no longer than the length of your toddler's arm. Show them how to carry a stick: away from their face and body, pointed down, and to never run with a stick.

continued →

6. Keep sharp scissors, knives, glue guns, and other potentially dangerous tools away from your toddler.

7. Use sunscreen during outdoor play. Bring a hat for sunny days.

8. Always have plenty of water and snacks available when heading outdoors.

9. Do a tick check after you have been outside. Check your child's entire body, specifically near their underarms, ears, inside the belly button, the backs of their knees, in and around their hair, and near the waist. If you find a tick attached to you or your child's body, remove it as soon as possible. (See Resources, page 81, for more information.)

10. Always learn about poisonous plants or animals in your area. Scout the area prior to an activity to make sure it is safe from poison ivy, poison oak, other poisonous plants, poisonous snakes or spiders, and any other threat in your locality.

11. Never pick flowers or plants from private property. Picking from public lands is illegal in some places. In general, keeping flowers intact for nature is the best approach for the health of the planet.

How to Use This Book

The activities in this book are mini adventures that encourage toddlers to explore and observe the natural world around them and develop early learning skills through play. You don't have to go far to be in nature. Your backyard or a local park will work just fine for most of the activities. If you don't have a backyard, exploring nature in your neighborhood is a great way to notice new things.

   The 50 activities in this book are divided among four chapters. You can do them in order, or flip to what interests you. Any materials needed for activities are easily accessible and are most likely items you already have in your house. An estimated prep time and a messiness rating are included to help you plan. Most activities should take 10, 15, or 20 minutes, though a few can be as brief as 5 minutes or as long as your toddler remains engaged. Each activity has a tip that shares a suggestion to adapt the activity to different situations.

   Let's get started!

CHAPTER 2

Fun with Nature All around Us: Weather, Seasons, and More

One of the first steps to learning about nature is to notice it: where it is, what it looks like, sounds like, smells like, feels like. These activities will encourage your toddler to use their senses to explore the outdoors and see that the world is filled with nature all around.

SKILLS
LEARNED

noticing and
identifying

classifying
and sorting

language and
vocabulary

ABC

Nature Scavenger Hunt

Toddlers love finding things! A nature scavenger hunt is an exciting way for them to learn about nature.

Messiness:

Prep time: 20 minutes

Activity time:
20 minutes

Materials
☐ Bucket
☐ Poster board
☐ Glue

Prep

Gather natural objects like pine cones, sticks, leaves, moss, and grass. Glue each natural object onto a poster board.

Steps

1. Head outside to a natural area.

2. Show the poster board to your toddler. Name the objects and ask them to look for them. Remind your toddler not to take anything from nature, but only to pick up pieces of nature that have fallen to the ground.

3. Give your toddler a bucket.

4. Place the poster where they can see it.

5. Walk around with your toddler as they hunt for each natural object on the board.

TIP: Do a nature scavenger hunt in every season. Label each board to mark the season and compare at the end of the year.

CAUTION: Avoid items that pose a choking risk.

Heading Out for a Hike

Hiking is an excellent way to experience nature. Remember to go big on fun and small on goals.

Messiness:
Prep time: 20 minutes
Activity time:
 30 minutes

Materials
- ☐ Water
- ☐ Snacks
- ☐ First aid gear
- ☐ Sunscreen
- ☐ Natural mosquito repellent and tick spray
- ☐ Hat

Prep

Pack up everything in the materials list. Head to a flat, safe hike for toddlers in your area.

Steps

1. Explain to your toddler that hiking just means walking in nature.

2. Choose a goal for the hike. This doesn't have to be too ambitious! You can choose a length—a 15-minute round-trip hike might be perfect—or you can choose a landmark to hike to, such as a waterfall or view.

3. Allow your toddler time to explore. Stop for water and snack breaks.

4. Ramp up the fun with a themed walk, such as critter spotting or finding trees with faces!

TIP: Let your toddler get as distracted as they want. The goal is to develop a love of being in nature.

CAUTION: Watch out for roots or uneven ground. Keep skin covered when in wooded areas to prevent tick bites, mosquito bites, or contact with poison ivy. Do a tick check on your toddler's body, paying close attention to tick hiding spaces, after the hike (see Safety First! page 5).

Rainy Day Puddle Stomping

Puddles are about as exciting as it can get for a toddler. One rainy day, let your toddler go wild stomping and splashing in the puddles left by the rain.

Messiness: ●●●
Prep time: 5 minutes
Activity time:
  20 minutes

Materials
☐ Raincoat
☐ Rain boots
☐ Umbrella

Prep
Find a sturdy stick outside. (It can be thin as long as it's sturdy.)

Steps
1. Help your toddler put on their rain gear.

2. Go outside and find some shallow puddles.

3. Take your stick and place it in the middle of the puddle. Mark the depth line with your finger as you pull the stick out of the puddle. Explain to your toddler that the part of the stick that was in the puddle shows the depth of the puddle.

4. If it's shallow enough (1 to 2 inches deep), show them how to jump over it or in it.

5. Play a game of follow the leader by jumping over puddles, making big or small splashes.

TIP: Your toddler can toss rocks into the puddle to see which ones make the biggest splash.

CAUTION: Always supervise your toddler when they are playing with or around water.

Noticing Nature on a Rainy Day

There is so much to take in on a rainy day! Take your child outdoors when it rains to let them explore this new world using all their senses.

Messiness:

Prep time: none

Activity time:
  30 minutes

Materials
☐ Raincoat
☐ Rain boots
☐ Umbrella

Steps

1. Help your toddler put on their rain gear.

2. Head outside. Ask your toddler to look around and notice how rain changes the outside world.

3. Ask them if they can see where the water is coming from. Where is it going?

4. Ask how the trees and plants look different in the rain. Have their colors changed?

5. Ask about sounds in the rain from raindrops or critters.

6. Talk about feelings on the skin such as chilly wind, heavy drops, or light spray.

7. Ask your toddler to look up at the clouds and see if they can spot any shapes in them.

TIP: Once inside, read a poem to your toddler about the rain.

Nature Obstacle Course

Use the elements of nature to help your toddler develop physical skills with a nature obstacle course.

Messiness: ✺✺✺

Prep time: 5 to 20 minutes

Activity time: 20 minutes

Materials

- ☐ Wooden boards (optional)
- ☐ Logs (optional)
- ☐ Small bridges (optional)
- ☐ Tree cookies (discs cut from tree trimmings) (optional)

Prep

Locate a natural area with elements such as small bridges, logs, and small hills.

If you have your own play space, create a nature obstacle course with a few natural elements, such as small bridges, tree cookies, inclines made of wooden boards, or logs to balance on.

Steps

1. Head outside to your nature course or to a natural area.

2. Point out the natural obstacles to your toddler.

3. Show them how to navigate the obstacles in a safe way.

TIP: A lumber yard might have scrap wood, but make sure it is sturdy without sharp edges or splinters.

CAUTION: Stay close by so your toddler doesn't stumble on logs, roots, or hills.

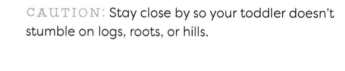

All Seasons Sensory Walk

Help your toddler develop their senses by heading out on a nature sensory walk.

Messiness: ✺ ✺
Prep time: none
Activity time:
  30 minutes

Materials
☐ Magnifying glass

Steps

1. Head outside to a park, your backyard, or any natural area.

2. Tell your toddler they are going to use their superpowers! These are amazing senses (sight, smell, touch, hearing) to help them learn about the world.

3. Invite them to explore nature with their senses (all except for taste!). Suggest they explore grass, leaves, trees, flowers, and pine cones. Show them how to look up close with the magnifying glass.

4. Help them describe colors, shapes, smells, and textures. Introduce words such as smooth, bumpy, fuzzy, prickly, and spongy.

5. Ask your toddler to listen to nature's sounds. Is it soft or loud? Do they hear patterns?

TIP: Try a sensory walk in the same place in different seasons.

CAUTION: As toddlers experience touch in nature, be vigilant so that they are not in danger of touching any poisonous plants like poison ivy or insects.

Reading about Nature in Nature

Enjoying a book outdoors is a simple activity that can help your toddler become more comfortable in nature.

Messiness:
Prep time: 5 minutes
Activity time:
 10 minutes

Materials
☐ Books
☐ Snacks
☐ Blanket
☐ Pillow

Prep

Pick some nature-themed books that relate to what your toddler can see outside. They might be about seasons or the plants and animals in your neighborhood. For inspiration, review our list of nature-themed books for toddlers (see Resources, page 81).

Steps

1. Ask your toddler to help you pack books and a favorite blanket and pillow.

2. Head outside and set up a comfortable reading nook together. You can use a hammock or make a nest with blankets and pillows.

3. Let the nature reading begin! Try to connect the theme of the book to what you can see in the outdoors. You might say, "The leaves in this picture are orange. What color are the leaves on that tree?"

TIP: Toddlers love books with bold illustrations, simple language, and great photos. Board books are always a hit.

Making a Nature Stick

A nature stick is a fun way to explore and to make a souvenir!

Messiness:
Prep time: none
Activity time:
  20 minutes

Materials

- ☐ Precut string or ribbon (6-inch pieces) or rubber bands

Steps

1. Go outside. Help your toddler pick out a sturdy stick without splinters or sharp, pointy edges, no bigger than the length of your toddler's arm.

2. Walk around, asking your toddler to point out what they see (a patch of flowers, a tree, a pond). This is their nature moment.

3. For each nature moment, they should search the area for a souvenir (leaf, pine cone, flower) to take home. Remind your toddler that they should only take objects that have already fallen to the ground.

4. Help them attach the nature moment souvenir to the stick with the ribbon or rubber bands.

TIP: Your toddler can continue to add to their nature stick during future outdoor adventures.

CAUTION: Instruct your toddler to walk with the stick pointing down, away from their body, and to never run with the stick.

Nature Impressions

Modeling clay is an excellent sensory activity for toddlers. Add nature objects, and you have a nature-full *and* sensory-full activity. If you'd prefer to use purchased clay rather than making your own, skip to step 3.

Messiness:

Prep time: none

Activity time:
  20 minutes

Materials

☐ Large mixing bowl
☐ Mixing spoon
☐ 4 cups flour
☐ 1 cup salt
☐ 1 cup warm water
☐ Small rolling pin
☐ Food coloring (optional)
☐ Airtight containers (for storing the clay)

Steps

1. With your toddler's help, use the mixing spoon to mix together the flour and salt in the mixing bowl. Add the water and food coloring (if using) and mix until it reaches a smooth consistency (a few lumps are okay).

2. Place the clay on a clean surface or plastic mat and knead it until smooth. Ask your toddler to give it a try.

3. Head outside. Ask your toddler to be on the lookout for nature objects with different textures such as pine cones, sticks, rocks, or tree bark.

4. At a table inside or outside, use the rolling pin to roll out the clay with your toddler until it is about ½ inch thick.

5. Show your toddler how to press each nature object gently but firmly into the clay until you have made an impression of the object.

6. Compare the different textures. Ask your toddler to match the impression with the object.

TIP: Separate your clay into batches in step 1 and mix into each batch a few drops of different colors of food coloring. Compare how the impressions look in different colors.

CAUTION: Avoid items that pose a choking risk to children.

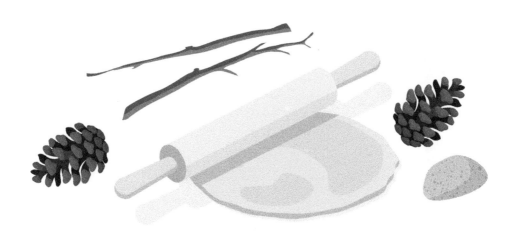

SKILLS
LEARNED

noticing and
identifying

classifying
and sorting

listening

language and
vocabulary

Nature Texture Surprise

Challenge your toddler's senses with this nature-object guessing game!

Messiness:

Prep time: 5 minutes

Activity time:
  20 minutes

Materials
☐ Shoebox
☐ Scissors

Prep
Cut an opening in the shoebox that is large enough for your child's hand to fit into.

Steps
1. Head outside and gather natural objects with a variety of textures: smooth (stone), rough (bark), prickly (pine cone), soft (moss), fuzzy (pussy willow).

2. Place the natural objects in the prepared box.

3. Ask your toddler to put their hand in the box and feel the objects. Tell them to use their super sense of touch to guess what the objects are inside.

4. After they've explored what's inside, ask them to pull out something fuzzy.

5. Repeat this several times, asking them to pull out different textures: smooth, rough, prickly, soft, etc.

TIP: Collect different-textured nature objects regularly when you are outside to have a stockpile ready for a rainy day!

CAUTION: Avoid selecting items that pose a choking risk to children.

Nature Fishing

Play nature fishing with nature objects to build your toddler's vocabulary and nature knowledge.

Messiness:
Prep time: none
Activity time:
  20 minutes

Materials
- ☐ Craft wire
- ☐ Stick
- ☐ Large bowl

Steps

1. Head outside and collect objects in nature that you can attach a wire to, such as pine cones, sticks, leaves, and bark. Objects like stones will be too slippery.

2. Secure wire to each object, making a large loop.

3. Wrap the craft wire around the stick, and form a "hook" by bending gently at the end.

4. Place all objects in a bowl.

5. Take turns trying to fish out a new object.

6. Ask your toddler to name the objects you each fish out. Talk with your toddler about each object.

TIP: Try this in different seasons and notice how many different objects you can find.

CAUTION: Avoid items that pose a choking risk to children.

Packing for a Picnic

Toddlers love to pack things up. This is a great activity to help them develop sorting skills!

Messiness:
Prep time: none
Activity time:
 20 minutes

Materials
- ☐ Lunch or snacks
- ☐ Picnic basket or bags
- ☐ Drinks
- ☐ Toys for outside
- ☐ Books
- ☐ Hat
- ☐ Blanket
- ☐ Bug spray
- ☐ Sunscreen

Steps

1. Tell your toddler you will be having a picnic outside, and you need their help to pack up.

2. Ask your toddler to help you make a list of everything you will need to be comfortable in the weather outside.

3. Ask them to help you make mini sandwiches and snacks.

4. Give them a bag or mini picnic basket and help them put food and drinks in one bag, and toys, clothing, and supplies in another.

5. Take it all outside and enjoy the picnic on a blanket. Follow up with nature-themed play.

TIP: Choose a theme for your picnic, such as "all things green" or "veggie day."

CHAPTER 3

Learning about Earth: Soil, Rocks, and Water

Anywhere you go outside, you're likely to come across rocks, soil, or water—which also happen to be some of nature's best tools for learning and playing. From painting with mud to the physics of rock stacking, the activities in this chapter will get your toddler's hands dirty with nature.

Cooking in the Mud Kitchen

Who says a kitchen shouldn't be messy? An outdoor mud kitchen will keep your toddler busy with creative play.

Messiness: ✿ ✿ ✿ ✿
Prep time: 10 minutes
Activity time:
  30 minutes

Materials

- ☐ Bucket
- ☐ Shovel
- ☐ Kitchen items such as spoons, muffin trays, bowls, cake tins
- ☐ Hand wipes
- ☐ Water (water bottle or other source)
- ☐ Change of clothes

Prep

Gather the materials in the bucket. Dress your toddler in clothing that you don't mind getting dirty. Have a change of clothes ready by the door for when you return home.

Steps

1. Tell your toddler you're going outside to make wonderful mud treats together!

2. Remind them that these are not food and are not to be eaten.

3. Head to your backyard or a local park. Find a spot with dirt (don't dig up grass) and a water source, if you need it.

4. Ask your toddler to dig up some mud and place it in the bucket. Using your water bottle and a spoon, help them make a mud mixture.

5. Ask your toddler to start baking! Ask them to make some treats such as mud muffins, pies, and cakes.

6. Keep cleanup easy by placing all items in the bucket. Wipe off any mud from your toddler. Leave messy clothes by the door when you return home so the mud stays outside.

TIP: Play the customer! Ask your toddler to pretend to be the baker and sell their treats to you.

SKILLS
LEARNED

imagination

cause and
effect

fine motor
skills

Mud Painting

Let your toddler unleash their inner Picasso in a super fun way with mud painting.

Messiness: 🌸 🌸 🌸 🌸

Prep time: 10 minutes

Activity time:
  20 minutes

Materials

- ☐ Shovel
- ☐ Bucket
- ☐ Wooden spoon
- ☐ Large piece of paper
- ☐ Paintbrush
- ☐ Hand wipes
- ☐ Water (water bottle or other source)
- ☐ Change of clothes

Prep

Gather your materials. Dress your toddler in clothing that you don't mind getting dirty. Have a change of clothes ready by the door for when you return home.

Steps

1. Head to an outdoor area with soil that can be dug up without destroying grass or other plantings. Soil near trees is usually a good area.

2. Ask your toddler to dig up some soil and place it in the bucket.

3. Make a mud mixture by adding water and mixing with a spoon.

4. Set up the paper on a flat spot on the ground.

5. Have your toddler dip the paintbrush in the mud and paint or splatter the mud on the paper.

6. Keep cleanup easy by placing all items in the bucket. Wipe off any mud from your toddler. Leave messy clothes by the door when you return home so the mud stays outside.

TIP: Show your toddler images of Jackson Pollock paintings as inspiration.

Water, Soil, and Rocks Sensory Bins

Explore nature using sight, touch, and smell with sensory bins.

Messiness: ✦ ✦ ✦
Prep time: 10 minutes
Activity time:
  10 minutes

Materials

- ☐ 3 tubs (about the size of a dishpan)
- ☐ Soil, sand, or clay
- ☐ Water

Prep

Head outside. Place the three tubs on flat ground or a table. Fill one with water and the second with soil, sand, or clay.

Steps

1. Ask your toddler to collect rocks for the third bin. Help them fill the bin with the rocks.

2. Allow your toddler to explore the materials in the three bins by looking, feeling, listening, and smelling. No tasting! Help them compare the items.

3. Let your toddler take as much time with the materials as they want.

TIP: Try out different materials in the bins such as leaves, grass, and pine needles.

CAUTION: Avoid items that pose a choking risk.

SKILLS
LEARNED

noticing and
identifying

asking
questions

listening

language and
vocabulary

ABC

Observing a Pond

Whether they are experiencing the sensation of mud between their fingers, listening to the calls of frogs, or watching dragonflies, there is so much for a toddler to experience at a pond!

Messiness:
Prep time: 10 minutes
Activity time:
  10 minutes

Materials
☐ Binoculars
☐ Water shoes
☐ Towel
☐ Bug spray
☐ Hat
☐ Sunscreen

Prep
Pack up the materials and travel to a pond.

Steps
1. Walk around the pond with your toddler to find a safe spot to watch what happens. Point out lily pads, frog sounds, turtles, dragonflies, and other insects or sounds.

2. At their chosen spot, have your toddler spend a few minutes just watching and listening. Tell them they will see more critters if they keep their movements small and their voice quiet. Show them how to get a close-up view with binoculars.

3. Ask your toddler if they would like to touch anything they see. Explain to your toddler that they can gently explore parts of the pond (such as plants) with touch as long as they are not disturbing the environment or hurting any creatures. They can wear their water shoes and get a closer look at the water's edge.

TIP: Read a book about pond life (see Resources, page 81).

CAUTION: Locate a pond that is safe and calm with no unsafe cliffs or edges. Keep a close eye on your child when exploring ponds. Be sure to check the wading area for slippery mud, algae, or grass, or sharp rocks and drop-offs. Water shoes will protect tender feet against sharp edges.

Rock Collecting and Categorizing

Toddlers love collecting things! The best part is that they are learning to organize and sort things when they do this.

Messiness:

Prep time: none

Activity time:
  20 minutes

Materials
- ☐ Bag
- ☐ Magnifying glass

Steps

1. Tell your toddler that today they are going to be a geologist, a person who studies rocks.

2. Head outside and gather as many rocks as you can together in your bag. A riverbed or a beach are good locations for rock collecting.

3. Show your toddler how to hold the magnifying glass close to the rock to see details. Ask them how the close-up view is different. Have them look for different colors, sheens, patterns, and shapes. Help them use descriptive vocabulary words.

4. Ask your toddler to group the rocks according to size, color, or shape.

TIP: Show your toddler pictures of different types of rocks so they can see the diversity in rocks.

CAUTION: Avoid collecting rocks that pose a choking risk.

Rock Stacking

Stacking rocks helps your toddler learn about balance and cause and effect. It can be one of their first physics experiments!

Messiness: ✹✹
Prep time: none
Activity time: 20 minutes

Materials
☐ None

Steps

1. Head to an outdoor place with many rocks of different sizes and shapes. Areas near rivers, the ocean, or quarries are excellent locations.

2. With your child, gather rocks of different sizes and shapes into a pile.

3. Demonstrate to your toddler how to stack the rocks.

4. Ask them to put one rock on top of the other to make a tower.

TIP: Disassemble the sculpture in a natural area, since critters rely on rocks for shelter and natural areas are protected by erosion.

CAUTION: Be very careful that your toddler does not crush or injure their fingers when stacking rocks. Avoid stacking rocks that pose a choking risk.

Rock Scrub

Toddlers love to take care of things. For this activity, they will take care of rocks, making them shiny and new!

Messiness:

Prep time: none

Activity time:
20 minutes

Materials
- ☐ Magnifying glass
- ☐ Bag
- ☐ Small scrubbing brush
- ☐ Container of water

Steps

1. Head outside. Help your toddler find a wide range of rocks.

2. Explain to your toddler that you're going to give the rocks a bath today.

3. Show your toddler how to brush off the dirt from each rock and wash it in the container filled with water.

4. Ask them how the rocks look and feel different now that they're clean. Help them use descriptive words.

5. Ask your toddler to group them according to size, color, or shape.

TIP: Bring a spray bottle of water with you when playing outside and let your toddler give rock baths anytime.

CAUTION: Avoid choosing rocks that pose a choking risk to children.

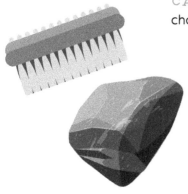

Wagon Haul

Hauling things from place to place puts a smile on any toddler's face.

Messiness: ✺✺✺✺✺
Prep time: 15 minutes
Activity time:
  20 minutes

Materials
- ☐ Safe, small wagon
- ☐ Shovel
- ☐ Chalk, signs, or stuffed animals (optional)

Prep

Prepare two piles of natural materials, such as dirt, leaves, or snow, a distance away from each other. One pile should be much bigger. This is the starting pile. Mark the pathway between the piles with chalk, signs, or stuffed animals.

Steps

1. Head to the hauling area with your toddler.

2. Explain to your toddler that they are going to load up the wagon from the starting pile of material, hauling it along the path to the ending pile of material. Show the start and end points.

3. Help your toddler load the material onto their wagon, make the journey, and then unload at the end.

TIP: Make the route more challenging by taking a trip up a small hill or through a puddle.

CAUTION: Supervise your child to make sure they do not eat any materials used in this activity or rub their eyes when handling nature objects.

SKILLS
LEARNED

noticing and
identifying

asking
questions

language and
vocabulary

ABC

Pond Water Sampling

Sampling pond water is an excellent way to see how ponds are brimming with life.

Messiness: ✺ ✺ ✺
Prep time: 5 minutes
Activity time:
  20 minutes

Materials
☐ Clean glass jar
  (about one gallon
  size, with lid)
☐ Knife or scissors
☐ Flashlight
☐ Magnifying glass

Prep
Carefully poke a few holes in the lid of the jar using a knife or scissors.

Steps
1. When you arrive at the pond, point out nature in and around the pond.

2. With your toddler safely on shore, collect some pond water in your jar. Seal it with the lid.

3. Back at home, look closely at the pond water you have collected together. Use the flashlight and magnifying glass to get different views.

4. Place the jar in a sunny window, away from the reach of your toddler. Check in on it every few days. Ask your toddler if they notice any changes.

TIP: Try this with sea water next time you visit the ocean.

CAUTION: Always keep a close eye on your child when exploring ponds. Rocks, mud, algae, and grass can make ponds very slippery.

Skipping Rocks

Throwing rocks in water is a great gross motor skill. Watching those ripples and water splat is hard to resist!

Messiness: ☀
Prep time: none
Activity time: 5 minutes

Materials
☐ None

Steps

1. Head outside to a calm and safe body of water without surf or waves. A small pond is ideal.

2. Gather large, safe-size rocks together.

3. Show your toddler how to throw a rock across the surface of the water to create a ripple.

4. Encourage your toddler to try different sizes of rocks. Ask which one goes farther.

TIP: If your toddler gets discouraged because they can't throw very far, start with puddles.

CAUTION: Always keep a close eye on your child when exploring ponds and playing with or around water.

Water Painting

Water painting is a great no-mess way for your toddler to explore their creativity.

Messiness: ✳
Prep time: none
Activity time:
  10 minutes

Materials
☐ Bucket
☐ Water
☐ Paintbrushes

Steps

1. Go outside on a warm day. Find an area with pavement or a sidewalk, or use the sides of your house for water painting.

2. Fill a bucket with water.

3. Ask your toddler to dip their paintbrushes in the water and paint any surface they want with the water.

4. Watch the design fade as the sun makes it go away.

TIP: Toddlers can draw lines and squiggles. This is perfectly fine! You can help your toddler with their picture.

CAUTION: Always supervise your toddler when they are playing with or around water.

Discovering Geodes

Geodes look like plain rocks from the outside, but inside they hold a secret: colorful crystals!

Messiness:
Prep time: 10 minutes
Activity time:
  20 minutes

Materials
- ☐ Geode kit
- ☐ Old sock
- ☐ Hammer

Prep

When your toddler is not looking, hide the geodes among other rocks in a natural space.

Steps

1. Tell your toddler that you will be hunting for geodes! Explain that geodes are special rocks with crystals inside.

2. Help your toddler search outside for the hidden geodes.

3. Once they have found them all, place a geode in the old sock. With your toddler a safe distance away, break open the geode using the hammer.

4. Look carefully inside together, noticing the crystals, colors, and patterns of the geode.

TIP: Starting a rock garden with the geodes and other large rocks is an excellent way for toddlers to explore geology.

CAUTION: Be very careful when using a hammer around your toddler. Do not let them use it or come close when you are breaking open the geodes.

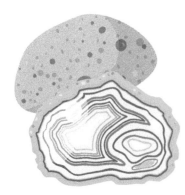

Quick and Easy Sandbox

Playing with sand is a wonderful sensory activity that stimulates creativity and imagination. You don't need a large sandbox. A small, portable one will do!

Messiness:
Prep time: 5 minutes
Activity time:
 20 minutes

Materials
- ☐ Small plastic tub (with lid for storage)
- ☐ Clean play sand (available online or at toy stores)
- ☐ Beach toys, such as watering cans, shovels, rakes, and buckets

Prep
Fill the tub with sand and fill the watering can with water.

Steps
1. Go outside to a space where your toddler can play with sand.

2. Show your toddler some ways to work with the sand, like mixing in water, raking it, and making houses or castles.

3. Let them have fun and work with the sand their way!

TIP: You can substitute sand with uncooked rice, dry beans, flaxseed, or chia seeds.

CAUTION: Supervise your child to make sure they do not eat the sand or rub sand in their eyes.

CHAPTER 4

Creatures and Critters: Birds, Bugs, and More

Toddlers just love animals. Helping your child see where and how animals live in their neighborhood is a wonderful way to connect them to nature and build vital tools, such as observational skills, fine motor skills, imagination, and language.

Animal Theater

Animal theater lets toddlers notice and imitate animals and gives their gross motor skills a boost!

Messiness:
Prep time: 10 minutes
Activity time:
  10 minutes

Materials
☐ Printer or magazines
☐ Index cards
☐ Glue
☐ Scissors

Prep

Print from the internet or cut from magazines small photos of animals in motion. Some ideas include a bird flying, a ladybug crawling, or a cricket jumping.

Steps

1. Head outside. Ask your toddler to notice how critters move. Point out birds flying, squirrels jumping, and insects crawling.

2. Tell your toddler you are going to play the "guess the animal" game.

3. Show them the printed photos.

4. Ask your toddler to help glue each photo to an index card.

5. Place the cards facedown and mix them up.

6. With your toddler, take turns turning over a card (being careful not to show it to the other player), acting out the animal and guessing what it is.

TIP: If you don't see critters outside, show your toddler videos of animals instead.

Making Tracks

Making tracks is a great sensory lesson for toddlers.

Messiness:

Prep time: None

Activity time:
  20 minutes

Materials
- ☐ Shovel
- ☐ Aluminum pan
- ☐ Water source

Steps

1. Go outside to a muddy place where animals live. The bank of a pond is a great place to look, but you can find tracks anywhere mud and animals are together.

2. Search for animal tracks together. Explain how tracks are made in mud when an animal steps.

3. Ask your toddler to dig up some dirt. Place it in the pan.

4. Add water to the dirt to make mud.

5. Show your toddler how to make a print by pressing down gently with their hand.

6. Set the print out to dry.

7. After it dries, ask your toddler how their print is different from other animal tracks.

TIP: Go on a track scavenger hunt! Use the printable in the Resources section of this book (page 81).

Bug Hunt

Finding bugs is one of the easiest nature activities you can do with your toddler.

Messiness:
Prep time: none
Activity time:
 20 minutes

Materials
☐ Magnifying glass

Steps

1. On a warm day, tell your toddler you're going out on a bug hunt! Head to a wooded or green area.

2. Explain that bugs like to hide. Show some typical hiding spots such as under logs and rocks, under leaves, on flower petals, under bark, or in grass.

3. Use a magnifying glass to get a closer look at the bugs.

TIP: Gently shake a flower over a piece of white paper to see what smaller bugs are hiding inside.

CAUTION: Not all bugs bite or sting, but some do, so make sure your toddler does not touch any insects unless you say it is okay.

Worms in the Rain

Most toddlers just love worms! Wait for a rainy day for this activity.

Messiness:
Prep time: none
Activity time:
  20 minutes

Materials
☐ Plastic bag or bucket
☐ Paper towels

Steps

1. Tell your toddler that you are going to find some worms.

2. Go outside and together look for worms on wet sidewalks or cement. Carefully gather a few in the bag or bucket.

3. Place a half-wet paper towel on a dry surface. Place the worms on the dry area of the paper towel.

4. Watch if they move toward the wet area of the paper towel.

5. After a few minutes of observing the worms, return them outside.

TIP: Have a worm race! See which worm makes its way to the wet part of the paper towel first.

CAUTION: Don't let your toddler put the worms in their mouth, and be sure to wash their hands after touching a worm.

SKILLS LEARNED

noticing and identifying	asking questions	listening	imagination	language and vocabulary
				ABC
🔍	❓	👂	💡	

Animal Home Tour

Toddlers love animals, and they love to play hide-and-seek! Combine the two with an animal home tour.

Messiness ✸
Prep time: 10 minutes
Activity time:
  30 minutes

Materials
☐ None

Prep

Do some online research to learn about local animals and their habitats.

Steps

1. Go outside. Tell your child you're going on an animal house tour.

2. As you walk around, point out places where animals make their homes. Make sure to point out bird nests, squirrel nests, and anthills. Point out holes in trees that are perfect for small mammals or birds, cracks in walls for chipmunks, and burrows or holes in the ground for rabbits or groundhogs.

3. Ask your toddler to find some animal homes!

TIP: With the use of blocks or other building materials, your toddler can make a home for one of their stuffed animals based on the animal homes they saw outside.

CAUTION: Don't let your toddler get too close to where an animal might be living or hiding.

Bird Sound Sleuth

Grow your toddler's observational skills with this fun introduction to bird sounds.

Messiness:
Prep time: 10 minutes
Activity time:
  20 minutes

Materials
☐ Device with internet

Prep

Research online videos of local types of birds making bird sounds. Your local parks department should be a good resource for discovering which birds live in your area. Birds such as songbirds, ducks, geese, raptors, and crows will provide a diverse range of sounds.

Steps

1. Watch the videos with your toddler. As you watch, talk about and name each bird. Imitate the bird sounds together.

2. Tell your toddler you are going to listen for these birds outside.

3. Go outside to an area with a large variety of birds such as a pond or a park.

4. Tell your toddler to listen carefully to the sounds around them.

5. Invite your toddler to imitate the bird sounds. Remind your toddler of the names of the birds they learned and the sounds they make.

TIP: Dusk is one of the best times to hear birds.

noticing and identifying	listening	fine motor skills	language and vocabulary
			ABC

Making a Pinecone Feeder

Making a pinecone bird feeder with your toddler is an easy, interactive project for your toddler to learn about birds.

Messiness:
Prep time: 5 minutes
Activity time:
  15 minutes

Materials
- ☐ String or twine
- ☐ Birdseed
- ☐ Nut butter or vegetable shortening
- ☐ Ice pop stick

Prep

Cut the string or twine into four 10-inch pieces.

Spread out the birdseed on a cookie sheet to reduce mess.

Steps

1. Head outside and ask your toddler to help find the biggest pine cones they can.

2. At a table inside or outside, tell your toddler you're going to make a yummy snack for the birds.

3. Attach a piece of cut string or twine to the top of each pine cone and make a loop.

4. Show your toddler how to spread the pine cone with nut butter or shortening using the ice pop stick.

5. Show your toddler how to roll the cone in birdseed.

6. Help your toddler hang their pinecone feeders on different branches of trees or bushes outside.

TIP: Keep feeders in a cool spot.

Building Nests

Making nests may be a challenge for a toddler, but with your help they can get a sense of how perfect these little homes are!

Messiness: 🌸🌸🌸

Prep time: none

Activity time:
30 minutes

Materials

- ☐ Twist ties
- ☐ Paper, cardboard, cotton scraps
- ☐ Glue gun

Steps

1. Go outside with your toddler in springtime and be on the lookout for bird's nests. When you see one, point it out to your toddler and talk about how birds use sticks, leaves, feathers, and fur to make nests that are homes for their babies. If it's not spring, you can look at photos online.

2. Tell your toddler you're going to make a nest now! Together, gather bendable items such as sticks, leaves, straw, long grass, vines, or willow fronds.

3. Show your toddler how to form a nest with the nature parts by bending the stronger loose parts, such as straw, sticks, or vines, into a circular shape.

4. Attach the ends using twist ties.

5. Add softer parts such as leaves, or indoor materials such as cotton or paper scraps.

6. Using a glue gun, glue the nest materials together, then let it dry.

TIP: Toddlers love little nooks and spaces of their own. Show them they can make their own nest out of blankets and pillows. They can pretend they are a bird!

CAUTION: Avoid items that pose a choking risk.

Making a Critter

This activity uses loose nature parts for your toddler to create their own critter!

Messiness: ✦✦

Prep time: none

Activity time: 20 minutes

Materials

- ☐ Bag
- ☐ Paper
- ☐ Glue

Steps

1. Spend some time looking at critters (birds, mammals, insects, amphibians, or reptiles) in books or online. Point out different body parts, such as wings, antennae, feet, legs, and beaks.

2. Go outside with your toddler to gather some natural building blocks in your bag. Gather stones, pine cones, leaves, seedpods, flower petals, twigs, pine needles, seeds, and berries.

3. Ask your toddler to arrange the nature parts into the shape of a critter on the piece of paper.

4. Glue the critter together.

5. Ask questions such as: Where does it live? What does it eat? How does it move?

TIP: Make a critter each time you go outside. Attach a ribbon to the top of each one and suspend the critters from a sturdy stick to make a critter mobile.

CAUTION: Avoid items that pose a choking risk.

Signs of Birds Scavenger Hunt

Being on the "hunt" for signs of birds will help develop your child's nature observation skills.

Messiness:

Prep time: 5 to 20 minutes

Activity time: 30 minutes

Materials

- ☐ Printer
- ☐ Photos of birds
- ☐ Paper (optional)
- ☐ Scissors (optional)
- ☐ Glue (optional)
- ☐ Crayon (optional)

Prep

Print the Signs of Birds Scavenger Hunt card (see Resources, page 81) or make your own scavenger hunt card.

To make your own, print out six to nine photos of birds flying, perching, drinking, swimming, eating, etc. Cut out the photos and then paste them onto a larger piece of paper.

Steps

1. Go outside with your toddler, show them the scavenger hunt card, and tell them you're going to go look for birds doing what they see in the photos.

2. Go to different areas to see different bird activities.

3. Once you and your toddler spot the activity, let them cross off each photo.

TIP: Adapt this activity for other themes, such as insects, leaves, or green objects.

Catching Butterflies

Catching real butterflies wouldn't be very easy for a toddler, or safe for a butterfly. This activity is the next best thing: making butterflies and then catching them in the air.

Messiness:

Prep time: none

Activity time:
25 minutes

Materials

- ☐ Small squares of tissue paper in different colors
- ☐ Yarn
- ☐ Butterfly net

Steps

1. If there are butterflies around, spend some time outside butterfly spotting with your toddler. Notice the colors and sizes of the butterflies you see. If you don't have butterflies outside, some museums or zoos have butterfly rooms or webcams (see Resources, page 81).

2. Once your toddler has a good idea of what butterflies looks like, tell them you are going to create some of your own.

3. Ask your toddler to select two colors of tissue paper for their butterfly.

4. Lay the pieces of tissue paper over each other, then tie the yarn in a knot around the middle. The tissue paper should fan out on either side of the knot.

5. Repeat step 4 to make more butterflies.

6. Head outside with the net and the butterflies in a bag.

7. One by one, throw the butterflies up in the air and ask your toddler to try to catch them with the net before they land on the ground.

TIP: Read *Butterfly, Butterfly, a Book of Colors* together (see Resources, page 81).

Creating a Bird Feeding Station

A bird feeding station is a perfect way for your child to care for back-yard birds.

Messiness:
Prep time: 5 minutes
Activity time:
  10 minutes

Materials
- ☐ Bird feeder
- ☐ Birdseed
- ☐ Binoculars (optional)
- ☐ Water (optional)

Prep

Locate a spot in your backyard where birds can safely come out to eat and not be in danger from predators or other threats. Ideally, your feeder will be in front of a window so your toddler has a front row seat. Set up the feeder.

Steps

1. Each morning, make a ritual of filling the feeder with your toddler.

2. Watch the birds that come to eat at the feeder. Use the binoculars to get a closer view.

3. If you have the space, add a water source. Birds need and appreciate clean water.

TIP: Keep the food going in all seasons. Backyard birds depend on reliable sources of food.

noticing and identifying	asking questions	language and vocabulary	SKILLS LEARNED
🔍	❓	**ABC**	

Raising Happy Butterflies

With a purchased butterfly kit, your child can watch caterpillars grow into butterflies over 5 to 10 days.

SEASONAL ACTIVITY

Messiness: ✳
Prep time: none
Activity time: 5 minutes

Materials
☐ Butterfly kit
☐ Fruit or sugar water

Steps

1. Follow your kit's instructions to set it up. This usually involves keeping the caterpillar cups upright with the lid on and out of direct sunlight.

2. With your toddler, watch the caterpillars crawl and eat.

3. In 5 to 10 days, the caterpillars will climb to the top of the cup and attach themselves to the lid of the cup. This means they are ready to transform into a chrysalis.

4. Move the disk with the chrysalis to the butterfly habitat, and closely follow your kit's instructions.

5. After a few weeks, the butterflies should emerge. Feed them slices of freshly cut fruit or sugar water for a few days.

6. Release your butterflies outside if it's over 50°F.

TIP: Read the book *The Very Hungry Caterpillar* when your toddler is watching this amazing metamorphosis take place!

CHAPTER 5

Green Growers: Flowers, Leaves, and Trees

One of the best things about trees is that they are always around! Noticing plants and trees and how they change from season to season is a lifelong nature lesson you can give your child. Flowers are one of the most beautiful gifts of nature and will attract any toddler's attention.

Growing a Miniature Garden

Growing plants with toddlers teaches them about nature and responsibility. When selecting seeds, try starting with radishes, lettuce, beans, peas, kale, or sweet potatoes. They are all easy to grow.

Messiness:
Prep time: 5 minutes
Activity time:
20 minutes

Materials
- ☐ Empty egg carton
- ☐ Toothpick
- ☐ Potting soil
- ☐ Seeds
- ☐ Aluminum tray

Prep

Remove the top from the egg carton. Using your toothpick, poke two tiny holes in the bottom of each cup for drainage.

Steps

1. Gather all your materials and head outside with your toddler.

2. Fill one hole in the egg carton two-thirds of the way full with potting soil. Ask your toddler to fill the rest of the holes.

3. Show your toddler how to gently place a few seeds on top, then sprinkle with soil. Keep the soil loose and crumbly.

4. Place the carton on a tray near a sunny window. Lightly water.

5. Ask your toddler to lightly water the garden every day.

TIP: Once the seedlings have grown, your toddler can transplant them to a larger pot in a windowsill, on a balcony, or outside. Just fill the container with more potting mix.

Pressing Flowers

Pressing flowers with your toddler in the warmer months will preserve them to enjoy for winter activities!

Messiness:

Prep time: none

Activity time:
  10 minutes

Materials

☐ 2 wooden boards (about the size of a book)
☐ Newspaper
☐ Cardboard (same size as boards)
☐ 1 (1-foot) piece of string

Steps

1. If you have an outdoor garden, gather a few flowers with your toddler. Otherwise, you can buy flowers at a market or find a farm where you and your toddler can pick flowers.

2. Have your toddler place one or two flowers (depending on how many will fit) on one wooden board. Cover the flower with newspaper, then the cardboard, then the second wooden board.

3. Tie the string around the bundle to secure it.

4. Wait several days, then check on the pressed flowers.

5. Notice what has changed about the flowers with your toddler.

TIP: Preserve the flower for nature study in cooler months or use it in a craft, such as making cards and bookmarks.

noticing and identifying	listening	cause and effect	fine motor skills	language and vocabulary
				**ABC**

Leaf Rubbings

A leaf rubbing is an easy and fun way for a toddler to study the parts of a leaf.

Messiness:

Prep time: none

Activity time:
20 minutes

Materials
- ☐ Crayons in different colors
- ☐ Tracing paper
- ☐ Clipboard (optional)

Steps

1. Head outside with your toddler and point out the many different shapes and colors of leaves you see.

2. Gather a few that your toddler chooses and ask them to look carefully and closely at the leaves.

3. At a table inside or outside, show your toddler how to peel the paper off a few different-colored crayons.

4. Place a piece of tracing paper in a clipboard (if using) and place the leaf between the paper and clipboard. If you're not using a clipboard, have your toddler place the paper gently on top of the leaf so it is not damaged.

5. Show your toddler how to make a rubbing of the leaf by carefully shading the tracing paper with the side of the peeled crayon.

TIP: Ask your toddler if they can match the parts of the tracing that show up most clearly to the original leaf.

Leaf Memory Game

This simple game will challenge your toddler's memory skills and help them learn about different types of leaves at the same time.

Messiness:
Prep time: none
Activity time:
  30 minutes

Materials
☐ Notecards
☐ Glue

Steps

1. Head outside with your toddler. Ask them to gather two "matching" leaves from four or five trees. Remind them to only pick leaves that are already on the ground.

2. At a table inside or outside, show your toddler how to glue each leaf to a notecard.

3. Once the cards are dry, turn each of them facedown and mix them up.

4. Take turns revealing a card and trying to locate its match.

5. When all matches are made, reshuffle and start again.

TIP: You can do this with other nature objects, such as seedpods, plants, or flowers.

CAUTION: Supervise your child and use glue that is nontoxic and safe.

noticing and identifying	asking questions	listening	imagination	fine motor skills	language and vocabulary	SKILLS LEARNED
					ABC	

Making Nature Crowns

Help your toddler make a crown of nature items in this fun and creative activity.

Messiness:
Prep time: 5 minutes
Activity time:
  25 minutes

Materials
☐ Construction paper
☐ Scissors
☐ Bag
☐ Glue or tape

Prep

Cut out strips of construction paper long enough to fit around your toddler's head. Toddlers with scissor skills can give this a try.

Steps

1. Head outside and ask your toddler to gather light nature objects, such as grass, leaves, flowers, sticks, tree bark, and moss, and place them in a bag. Remind your toddler to only pick parts of nature that have fallen to the ground.

2. Help your toddler glue or tape the nature objects to the construction paper strips.

3. Tape the ends of the crown and help your toddler place it on their head.

TIP: Your toddler can continue to add objects to the crown each time they explore outside.

CAUTION: Avoid items that pose a choking risk.

Name That Smell

It's true that we should stop more often to smell the flowers (or herbs). This game helps develop your toddler's senses, language, and nature identification skills.

Messiness:
Prep time: none
Activity time:
  20 minutes

Materials

☐ 4 small plastic or glass containers such as mason jars
☐ Tape
☐ Marker
☐ Fabric (for a blindfold)

Steps

1. Head outside with your toddler to your garden or a farmers' market. Gather herbs and flowers.

2. At a table inside or outside, write each plant's name on a piece of tape with a marker and place it on the container.

3. Ask your toddler to smell each herb or flower. Help them place each plant into its own container, and identify each plant for them.

4. Place a blindfold over your toddler's eyes.

5. Have your toddler smell each container and guess the herb or flower.

TIP: If you have selected herbs that are safe to taste, such as dill, oregano, or parsley, repeat this as a taste test.

CAUTION: Research your herbs well and ensure your child is not allergic. Not all herbs are safe for children. St. John's wort and chamomile may cause adverse reactions in children.

Making Tree Faces

Made from mud and simple objects found in nature, tree faces are a fun way for a toddler to see a tree a little differently.

Messiness: ✹✹✹✹

Prep time: none

Activity time:
25 minutes

Materials
- ☐ Trowel, small spade, or other mixing tool
- ☐ Bucket
- ☐ Water
- ☐ Hand wipes
- ☐ Change of clothes

Steps

1. Dress your toddler in clothes and shoes that are suitable for messy play and head outside to an area with trees.

2. Ask your toddler to look around and pick out a tree that looks like it's smiling or frowning.

3. Ask them to gather natural materials to help create a face. They can pick up acorns, leaves, moss, sticks, rocks, or feathers. The rule, as always, is that it should already be on the ground.

4. With the trowel or spade, help your toddler dig a hole past the topsoil, about 2 to 8 inches deep. Help them fill their bucket about halfway with the soil, then add enough water to make claylike mud.

5. Help your toddler take handfuls of mud and form it into a face shape on the tree trunk. Choose a spot that is free of insects, holes, or otherwise not in use by living critters. Also, make sure there is no poison ivy or other poisonous plant near the space.

6. After they have formed the shape of their face, have them add the natural objects for eyes, nose, mouth, hair, horns, warts, antennae, or whatever they like!

7. Wipe off any mud from your toddler. Leave messy clothes by the door when you return home so mud stays outside.

TIP: Let the face harden and visit it with your toddler again!

CAUTION: Avoid items that pose a choking risk.

SKILLS
LEARNED | noticing and
identifying | language and
vocabulary

$\mathbb{Q}$ | **ABC**

Becoming a Tree Friend

Befriending a tree is a great way for your toddler to learn about how it changes from season to season.

Messiness:

Prep time: none

Activity time:
10 minutes

Materials

☐ None

Steps

1. Go outside to a local, familiar area with trees and ask your toddler to look around.

2. Tell them that trees need us to be their friends. Ask them to choose one tree to make their friend.

3. Walk over to the tree with your toddler. Ask them to look at their tree. Ask them what they notice that makes this tree different. What do they like about it? Do they think it is happy? Help them use new vocabulary to describe the tree.

4. Take your toddler to visit their tree friend regularly in different seasons.

TIP: Your toddler can decorate the tree with pinecone feeders (page 50).

Making an Outdoor Mural

An outdoor mural is a great way for your toddler to create art (and leave the mess outside). Being on the hunt for nature objects will help them tune up their nature IQ!

Messiness:
Prep time: none
Activity time:
  30 minutes

Materials
- ☐ Bag or bucket
- ☐ Large sheet of paper
- ☐ Glue

Steps

1. Head outside with your toddler and gather natural materials such as leaves, flowers, moss, sticks, rocks, or feathers. The rule, as always, is that it should already be on the ground.

2. Help your toddler glue their nature treasures onto the paper to create a nature collage. They can make a pattern or a picture—whatever they'd like!

TIP: As an alternative to regular paper, use contact paper and stick nature objects directly onto it.

CAUTION: Avoid items that pose a choking risk.

Making Leaf People

Leaves are a plentiful and diverse part of nature! Let your toddler's imagination run wild by creating fun people from leaves.

Messiness:

Prep time: none

Activity time:
20 minutes

Materials

☐ Paper
☐ Glue
☐ Crayons

Steps

1. Head outside with your toddler. Ask them to notice how many different leaves there are.

2. Tell them to choose a selection of colors, shapes, and sizes to make up leaf people. They should think about how the leaf will form different body shapes.

3. At a table inside or outside, show your toddler how to position the leaves to make leaf people.

4. Help your toddler glue the leaves to paper.

5. Ask them to draw arms, legs, and faces on their leaf people!

TIP: Help your toddler create stories and poems about their leaf people.

Exploring Seeds

Toddlers love to play with food. This activity helps them learn about the importance of seeds to make more fruits and vegetables.

Messiness:
Prep time: none
Activity time:
  10 minutes

Materials
☐ Fruits and vegetables
☐ Knife
☐ Cutting board

Steps

1. With clean hands, help your toddler gather an assortment of fruits and vegetables, such as apples, pears, tomatoes, and cucumbers.

2. Cut each one in half on your cutting board, and show your toddler that each has seeds inside.

3. Ask them to use their sense of touch and sight to compare the shapes, colors, and sizes of the seeds.

4. Explain to your toddler that seeds help create new fruits and vegetables.

5. Eat the cut fruits and vegetables!

TIP: Read a book about gardening together.

CAUTION: Be very careful when using a knife around your toddler.

Growing Roots from Foods We Eat

Regrowing food from the pit of a food we've eaten is a miracle of nature. Introduce this to your toddler with a familiar food: avocado.

Messiness: ✴
Prep time: none
Activity time:
  10 minutes

Materials
☐ Avocado pit
☐ Toothpicks
☐ Small glass

Steps

1. Together with your toddler, examine an avocado pit. Tell your toddler you're going to use this pit to grow more avocados.

2. Stick toothpicks into the pit. Suspend the pit on the rim of a glass of water, using the toothpicks for support.

3. Watch for the next few weeks as roots develop. Explain to your toddler that roots help gather food and water for the growing plant.

4. When the seed sprouts roots, transplant the rooted pit to your garden!

TIP: Try this activity with sprouted garlic cloves by placing the sprouted clove in a clear container and filling it with water.

CAUTION: Be very careful when using toothpicks with your toddler. Do not let them play with them.

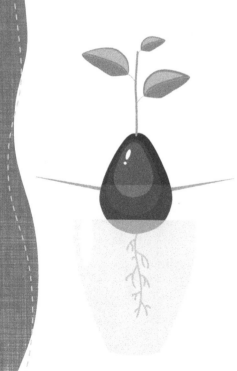

Resources

BOOKS

Baby Bear Sees Blue by Ashley Wolff
Like a toddler, Baby Bear learns about the natural world by asking lots of questions. He also explores using his senses, making this an excellent book for sensory exploration.

Butterfly, Butterfly, a Book of Colors by Petr Horáček
With peek-through die cuts and pop-up surprises, this fun and colorful book teaches toddlers about the many types of insects.

Little White Rabbit by Kevin Henkes
The adventurous little white rabbit explores the outdoor world, wondering what it would be like to be different. Excellent for the nature-curious toddler.

Pond Walk by Nancy Elizabeth Wallace
Toddlers will love following along as Buddy and his mother spend a relaxing day at the pond, learning about the animals, bugs, and plants that live there.

Step Gently Out by Helen Frost
A poem that reveals how you can see nature more closely if you slow down and observe more carefully.

The Very Hungry Caterpillar by Eric Carle
This children's classic is often a child's first introduction to insects and metamorphosis.

What's in My Garden?: A Book of Colors by Cheryl Christian
This lift-the-flap board book helps toddlers and babies develop fine motor skills and learn to name the colors of fruits and vegetables.

WEBSITES

AllTrails.com
A source for great trail hikes that are rated by hikers and organized by difficulty.

American Academy of Pediatrics, "How to Remove a Tick," healthychildren. org/english/health-issues/conditions/from-insects-animals/pages /how-to-remove-a-tick.aspx#

Butterfly Webcam, Melbourne Zoo, Australia
youtube.com/watch?v=lKOIqNGcW-M

ChildhoodByNature.com
This is author Jenette Restivo's website, and it is filled with many ideas for raising children with nature.

PRINTABLE ACTIVITIES

Making Tracks Printable
childhoodbynature.com/the-nature-for-toddlers-activity-book -additional-resources

Signs of Birds Scavenger Hunt Printable
childhoodbynature.com/the-nature-for-toddlers-activity-book -additional-resources

References

Beery, Thomas, Louise Chawla, and Peter Leven. "Being and Becoming in Nature: Defining and Measuring Connection to Nature in Young Children." *International Journal of Early Childhood Environmental Education* 7, no. 3 (Summer 2020), 3–22.

Glassy, Danette. "Playing Outside: Why It's Important for Kids." healthychildren.org. Last updated April 28, 2022. healthychildren.org /english/family-life/power-of-play/Pages/playing-outside-why -its-important-for-kids.aspx

Hanscom, Angela J. *Balanced and Barefoot.* New Harbinger Publications, 2016.

Louv, Richard. *Last Child in the Woods.* Algonquin Books, 2008.

Monti, Fiorella, Roberto Farné, Fabiola Crudeli, Francesca Agostini, Marianna Minelli, and Andrea Ceciliani. "The Role of Outdoor Education in Child Development in Italian Nursery Schools. *Early Child Development and Care* 189, no. 6 (2017). doi.org/10.1080/03004430.2017.1345896

Morrissey, Anne-Marie, Caroline Scott, and Llewellyn Wishart. "Infant and Toddler Responses to a Redesign of Their Childcare Outdoor Play Space." *Children, Youth and Environments* 25, no. 1 (2015), 29–56. doi.org /10.7721/chilyoutenvi.25.1.0029

Acknowledgments

I would like to thank my children, Zane and Calvin, for being wonderful, kind, nature-loving boys. You inspire me because you are always willing to take on a new adventure outdoors—wherever that may be. I am also grateful for my husband, Adam, who has been the ideal partner to raise children with a love for the natural world.

I would like to thank Callisto Media for the opportunity to share these ideas so more children can explore the nature around them. And, I'd like to thank each of you for your desire to raise your child with nature, for their future and the planet.

About the Author

 **Jenette Restivo** is a writer, mother, and nature devotee. She founded the website childhoodbynature.com to help parents and caregivers raise young naturalists. Jenette is a former content strategist for the Children & Nature Network. She has written and produced television programs for ABC, CBS, National Geographic, and the History Channel, among others. She is trained in ornithology and is determined to learn dendrology next because she is in love with trees.